*Higher
Consciousness*

By C. W. Leadbeater

Copyright © 2021 Lamp of Trismegistus. All rights reserved. No part of this publication may be reproduced or transmitted in any form or by any means, electronic or mechanical, including photocopying, recording, or by any information storage and retrieval system, without permission in writing from Lamp of Trismegistus. Reviewers may quote brief passages.

ISBN: 978-1-63118-591-5

Esoteric Classics

Other Books in this Series and Related Titles

The Hymns of Hermes by G R S Mead (978-1-63118-405-5)

Clairvoyance and Psychic Abilities by A Besant &c (978-1-63118-403-1)

Gnosis of the Mind by G R S Mead (978-1-63118-408-6)

Freemasonry and the Egyptian Mysteries by C. W. Leadbeater (978-1-63118-456-7)

Rosicrucian Rules, Secret Signs, Codes and Symbols by various (978-1-63118-488-8)

An Outline of Theosophy by C W Leadbeater (978-1-63118-452-9)

Paracelsus, the Four Elements and Their Spirits by M P Hall (978-1-63118-400-0)

Essays on Ancient Magic by Helena P Blavatsky (978-1-63118-535-9)

Essays on the Esoteric Tradition of Karma by A Besant &c (978-1-63118-426-0)

The Use of Evil by Annie Besant (978-1-63118-532-8)

Occult Arts by William Q. Judge (978-1-63118-559-5)

The Alchemical Catechism of Paracelsus by Paracelsus (978-1-63118-513-7)

Alchemy in the Nineteenth Century by Helena P Blavatsky (978-1-63118-446-8)

Qabbalistic Teachings and the Tree of Life by M P Hall (978-1-63118-482-6)

The Historic, Mythic and Mystic Christ by Annie Besant (978–1–63118–533–5)

The Hidden Mysteries of Christianity by Annie Besant (978–1–63118–534–2)

The Brotherhood of Religions by Annie Besant (978–1–63118–563–2)

The Religion of Theosophy by Bhagwan Das (978–1–63118–565–6)

Arcane Formulas or Mental Alchemy by W W Atkinson (978-1-63118-459-8)

The Machinery of the Mind by Dion Fortune (978-1-63118-451-2)

The Leadbeater Reader: A Selection of Occult Essays (978-1-63118-483-3)

Audio versions are also available on Audible, Amazon and Apple

Other Books in this Series and Related Titles

Theories About Reincarnation and Spirits by H P Blavatsky (978–1–63118–590–8)

The Use and Power of Thought by C W Leadbeater (978–1–63118–589–2)

Commentary on the Pymander by G R S Mead (978–1–63118–588–5)

Hypnotism and Mesmerism by Annie Besant (978–1–63118–587–8)

Spirits of Various Kinds by Helena P Blavatsky (978–1–63118–586–1)

The Hidden Language of Symbolism by Annie Besant (978–1–63118–585–4)

Eastern Magic & Western Spiritualism by Henry S Olcott (978–1–63118–584–7)

Spiritual Progress and Practical Occultism by H P Blavatsky (978–1–63118–583–0)

Memory and Consciousness by Besant & Blavatsky (978–1–63118–582–3)

The Origin of Evil by Helena P Blavatsky (978–1–63118–581–6)

The Camp of Philosophy: Studies in Alchemy by Bloomfield (978–1–63118–580–9)

The Testaments of the Twelve Patriarchs (978–1–63118–579–3)

Occult or Exact Science? by Helena P Blavatsky (978–1–63118–578–6)

Occultism, Semi-Occultism & Pseudo Occultism by A Besant (978–1–63118–577–9)

The Fourth-Gospel and Synoptical Problem by G R S Mead (978–1–63118–576–2)

On the Bhagavad-Gita by T Subba Row &c (978–1–63118–575–5)

What Theosophy Does for Us by C W Leadbeater (978–1–63118–574–8)

Spiritual Life for Man by Annie Besant (978–1–63118–573–1)

The Mysteries by Annie Besant (978–1–63118–572–4)

Fundamental Ideas of Theosophy by Bhagwan Das (978–1–63118–571–7)

Dreams: What They Are and Caused by C W Leadbeater (978–1–63118–570–0)

Audio versions are also available on Audible, Amazon and Apple

Table of Contents

Introduction...7

Higher Consciousness...9

Buddhic Consciousness...39

INTRODUCTION

The word "esoteric" can be difficult to define. Esotericism in general can be seen less as a system of beliefs and more as a category, which encompasses numerous, different systems of beliefs. It's a bit of juxtaposition, since the word "esoteric" indicates something that few people know about, while the term itself broadly covers numerous philosophies, practices, areas of study and belief systems.

In a greater sense, Esotericism acts as a storehouse for secret knowledge, which is often considered ancient (by *tradition, if not by fact*), passed down from generation to generation, in private. At various times in history, simply possessing the knowledge of some of these subjects, was considered illegal and a jailable offence, if discovered. This usually included such general topics as Alchemy, Pharmacology, Qabalah, Hermeticism, Occultism, Ceremonial Magic, Astrology, Divination, Rosicrucianism and so on. Collectively, these areas of study were often referred to as the esoteric sciences.

Sometimes, the outer garment of a subject isn't esoteric, while what is hidden beneath it, is. As an example, Freemasonry isn't necessarily esoteric by nature (at *least not anymore*), but certain signs, passwords and handshakes given to the candidate during their initiation, are in fact, esoteric, in the sense that they are hidden from the general public.

Today, in the twenty-first century, such topics are readily available at bookstores across the country, and numerous mainsteam publishers offer beginners guides and coffee-table volumes on many of these subjects, intended for mass appeal. Books like *"The Secret"* have turned previously arcane topics into household knowledge. All that being the case, however, it isn't to say that there still aren't buried secrets to uncover, ancient wisdom being ignored and forgotten mysteries to be explored. In fact, it is often that we are only able to further our own studies by standing on the shoulders of these disappearing giants.

Lamp of Trismegistus is doing its part to help preserve humanity's esoteric history by making some of these classics available to those students who are seeking to unearth the knowledge of these ancient colossi.

So, be sure to check other titles from our *Esoteric Classics* series, as well as our *Occult Fiction*, *Theosophical Classics*, *Foundations of Freemasonry Series*, *Supernatural Fiction*, *Paranormal Research Series*, *Studies in Buddhism* and our *Christian Apocrypha Series*. You can also download the audio versions of most of these titles from Amazon, Apple or Audible, for learning on the go.

HIGHER CONSCIOUSNESS

Students who have not yet experienced the buddhic consciousness - consciousness in the intuitional world - frequently ask us to describe it. Efforts have been made in this direction, and many references to this consciousness and its characteristics are to be found scattered through our literature; yet the seeker after knowledge finds these unsatisfactory, and we cannot wonder at it.

The truth is that all description is necessarily and essentially defective; it is impossible in physical words to give more than the merest hint of what this higher consciousness is, for the physical brain is incapable of grasping the reality. Those who have read Mr. Hinton's remarkable books on the fourth dimension will remember how he tries to explain to us our own limitations with regard to higher dimensions, by picturing for us with much careful detail the position of an entity whose senses could work in two dimensions only. He proves that to such a being the simplest actions of our world must be incomprehensible. A creature who has no sense of what we call depth or thickness could never see any terrestrial object as it really is; he could observe only a section of it, and would therefore obtain absolutely wrong impressions about even the commonest objects of everyday life, while our powers of motion and of action would be utterly incomprehensible to him.

The difficulties which we encounter in trying to understand the phenomena even of the astral world are precisely similar to those which Mr. Hinton supposes to be experienced by his two-dimensional entity; but when we try to raise our thoughts to the intuitional world we have to face a state of existence which is lived in no less than six dimensions, if we are to continue at that level to employ the same nomenclature. So I fear we must admit from the outset that any attempt to comprehend this higher consciousness is foredoomed to failure; yet, as is but natural, the desire to try again and again to grasp something of it arises perennially in the mind of the student. I do not venture to think that I can say anything to satisfy this craving; the utmost that one can hope is to suggest a few new considerations, and perhaps to approach the subject from a somewhat different point of view.

The Monad in its own world is practically without limitations, at least as far as our solar system is concerned. But at every stage of its descent into matter it not only veils itself more and more deeply in illusion, but it actually loses its powers. If in the beginning of its evolution it may be supposed to be able to move and to see in an infinite number of these directions in space which we call dimensions, at each downward step it cuts off one of these, until for the consciousness of the physical brain only three of them are left. It will thus be seen that by this involution into matter we are cut off from the knowledge of all but a minute part of the worlds which surround us; and furthermore, even what is left to us is but imperfectly seen. Let us make an effort to realise what the higher consciousness may be by gradually supposing away some of our limitations; and although we are labouring under them even while we are thus supposing, the effort may possibly suggest to us some faint adumbration of the reality.

Let us begin with the physical world. The first thing that strikes us is that our consciousness, even of that world, is curiously imperfect. The student need feel no surprise at this, for he knows that we are at present only just beyond the middle of the fourth round, and that the perfection of consciousness of any plane will not be attained by normal humanity until the seventh round. The truth is that our whole life is imprisoned within limitations which we do not realise only because we have always endured them, and because the ordinary man has no conception of a condition in which they do not exist. Let us take three examples; let us see how we are limited in our senses, our powers and our intellect respectively.

First, as to our senses. Let us take the sense of sight for an example, and see how remarkably imperfect it is. Our physical world consists of seven sub-planes or degrees of density of matter, but our sight enables us to perceive only two of these with anything approaching perfection. We can usually see solid matter, if it is not too finely subdivided; we can see a liquid that is not absolutely clear; but we cannot see gaseous matter at all under ordinary conditions, except in the rare instances in which it has an especially brilliant colour (as in the case of chlorine) or when it happens to be dense, to be much compressed, and to be moving in a particular way - as in the case of the air which may sometimes be seen rising from a heated road. Of the four etheric subdivisions of physical matter we remain absolutely unconscious so far as sight is concerned, although it is by means of the vibration of some of these ethers that what we call light is conveyed to the eye.

Let us then commence the imaginary process of removing our limitations by considering what would be the effect if we really possessed fully the sight of the physical world. I am not taking into consideration the possibility of any increase in the *power* of our sight, though no doubt that also will come in due course, so that we shall be able so to alter the focus of the eye as to make it practically a telescope or a microscope at will. I am thinking for the moment only of the additional objects that would come into our view if our sight were perfected.

Nothing would any longer be opaque to us, so that we could see through a wall almost as though it were not there, and could examine the contents of a closed room or of a locked box with the greatest ease. I do not mean that by etheric sight a man could see through a mountain, or look straight through the earth to the other side of it; but he could see a good way into the rock, and he could see down to a considerable depth in the earth, much as we can now see through many feet of water to the bottom of a clear pool.

One can readily see a score of ways in which the possession of such a faculty would be practically valuable, and it would manifestly add to our knowledge in many directions. All surgical work could be performed with an ease and certainty of which at present we have no conception, and there would be fewer cases of inaccurate diagnosis. We could see the etheric bodies of our friends, and so we should be able to indicate unfailingly the source and cause of any nervous affection. A whole fresh world would come under the observation of the chemist, for he would then be able to deal with ethers as he now deals with gases. Our sight would instantly inform us as to the healthiness or otherwise of our surroundings, just as even now our noses warn us of the presence of certain forms of putrefaction. We could see at once when we were in the presence of undesirable germs or impurities of any kind, and could take our precautions accordingly. We could study the great hosts of the fairies, of the gnomes and the water-spirits, as readily as now we can study natural history or entomology; the world would be far fuller and far more interesting with even this slight augmentation of our sense.

But remember that even this would not take us beyond the physical world; it would simply enable us to see that world more fully. We should still be liable to deception, we should still be capable of error with regard to the thoughts and feelings of others. We should still be blind to all the most beautiful part of the life which surrounds us, even though we should see so much more of it than we do now. But even with the fullest physical sight we could see nothing as it really is, but only, at most, what corresponds to a looking-glass reflection of it. The two-dimensional entity could never see a cube; he would be quite incapable of imagining such a thing as a cube, and the nearest he could come to its comprehension would be to see a section of it as a square. However difficult it may be for us to grasp such an idea, we are at the present moment seeing only a section of everything that surrounds us; and because that is so, we think many things to be alike which are in reality quite different - just as to the two-dimensional creature the thinnest sheet of metal would appear precisely the same as a heavy block of it, the base of which had the same shape and area.

Then as to our powers. Here also we are strangely limited. However strong a man may be, however clever he may be at his speciality, whether that speciality be physical or mental, he can never work at it beyond a certain strictly limited extent without beginning to suffer from fatigue. Most people do not realise that this fatigue is always and entirely a physical disability. We speak of the mind as tired; but the mind cannot be tired; it is only the physical brain through which that mind has to express itself that is capable of fatigue. And even when the man is fresh and strong, how great are the difficulties in the way of a full expression of his thought! He has to try to put it into words; but words are feeble things at best, and can never really convey what the man feels or thinks; they are often misinterpreted, and the impression that they give is generally not at all what the speaker or writer originally intended.

The physical body is a serious obstacle in the way of rapid locomotion. Wherever we wish to go we have to carry with us this dense vehicle, this heavy lump of clay, that weighs the man down and checks his progress. At great expense and discomfort we must convey it by train or by steamer; and even with all our latest inventions, and with the wonderful progress that has been made with regard to all means of transportation, what a difficulty is this question of physical distance! How it stands in the way of the acquisition of knowledge; how it troubles the heart and lacerates the feelings of separated friends! The moment that we are able to raise our consciousness into a higher world all these difficulties are transcended.

Then as to our intellect. We are in the habit of boasting of it as some great thing. We speak of the march of intellect, of its great development, and generally speaking regard it as something of which we may reasonably be proud. Yet the truth is that it is nothing but a ridiculous fragment of what it presently will be - a fact which is abundantly clear to those of us who have had the privilege of coming into contact with some of the Masters of the Wisdom, and seeing in Them what a fully developed intellect really is. Here again our studies ought to save us from the common error, for we know that it is the fifth round in each chain which is specially devoted to the development of the intellectual faculties; and as we are still in the fourth we naturally cannot expect that they should as yet be at all fully unfolded. In fact, at this stage they would be scarcely unfolded at all, if it were not for the stupendous stimulus that was given to the evolution of humanity by the descent of the Lords of the Flame from Venus in the middle of the Third Root Race.

All this is true; the physical consciousness is sadly limited; but how are we to transcend it? It might seem that in the ordinary process of evolution we ought to perfect the physical senses before we acquire those of the astral world; but our powers do not unfold themselves exactly in that way. In order that the man shall be able to function in his physical body at all, there must be an uninterrupted connection between the ego and that vehicle; and this involves the existence of the mental and astral bodies. At first they are employed chiefly as bridges across which communication passes; and it is only as our development progresses that they come into use as separate vehicles. But inevitably while the consciousness is sending down messages through them, and receiving in return impressions through them, they become to a certain small extent awakened; so that even in a savage, who cannot be said to have any consciousness worth speaking of outside of the physical vehicle, there is yet a faint dawning of intellect and often a considerable amount of emotion. At the stage where the ordinary man of civilised countries stands at the present moment, his consciousness is on the whole more centred in his astral body than in the physical, even though it is true that the powers of the physical are as yet by no means fully unfolded. Their stage of unfoldment corresponds to the round in which we are now engaged; at this period only a partial development can be expected, but that partial development shows itself to some extent in the mental and astral bodies, as well as in the purely physical.

A good deal can be done even with the physical body by careful training, but much more can be done in proportion with the astral and mental bodies, the reason being that they are built of finer matter and so are much more readily amenable to the action of thought. Even the physical body may be greatly affected by that action, as is shown by the remarkable performances of faith-healers and Christian Scientists, and also by the well-authenticated examples of the appearance of the stigmata upon the bodies of some of those who have meditated strongly upon the alleged crucifixion of the Christ. But while only the few by determined exercise of thought-power can succeed in thus moulding the physical vehicle; anyone may learn how to control both the astral and the mental bodies by this power.

This is one of the objects which we seek to gain by the practice of meditation, which is the easiest and safest method of unfolding the higher consciousness. A man works steadily at his meditation year in and year out, and for a long time it seems to him that he is making no headway; yet all the while in his steady upward striving he is wearing the veil between the planes thinner and thinner, and at last one day there comes the moment when he breaks through and finds himself in another world. So wondrous, so transcendent, is that experience that he exclaims with startled delight:

"Now for the first time I really live; now at last I know what life means! I have thought before that life on the physical plane could sometimes be fairly keen and brilliant - yes, even vivid and full of bliss; but now I realise that all that was the merest child's play - that even in my most exalted moments I had no comprehension, no faintest suspicion of the glorious reality."

And yet all this, which the man feels so intensely when for the first time he touches the astral world, will be repeated with still stronger force of contrast when he transcends that world in turn, and opens himself out to the influences of the mental level. Then again he will feel that this is his first glimpse of actuality, and that even the most wonderful incidents of his astral life were to this but "as moonlight unto sunlight and as water unto wine". Again and again this happens to him as he climbs the ladder of evolution and comes nearer and nearer to reality; for verily it is true, as the old books have said, that "Brahman is bliss", and ever as one approaches the realisation of Him that bliss increases.

But the higher the joy the greater the contrast between the inner life and the life of the physical world; so that to return from that to this seems like sinking into a profound abyss of darkness and despair. The contrast is indeed great; so great that one cannot wonder that many of the saints of old, having once tasted this higher bliss, forsook all in order to follow it, and retired to cave or to jungle that there they might devote themselves to this higher life, in comparison with which all else that men hold valuable seems but as dust before the wind. I remember that, in the early days of this Society, we were told in one of the letters which came through Madame Blavatsky that when an adept had spent a long time in the nirvanic consciousness (leaving his body in a trance for weeks together), when he came back again into physical life he found the contrast so severe that he fell into a black depression which lasted for many days. Our terms were used very loosely in those days, and in this case the word adept must have referred to some one in the early stages of occult development - an adept merely in the sense that he was sufficiently accustomed to occult gymnastics to be able to leave his body and reside for a time upon a somewhat higher level - not what we now mean by nirvana, for only a real Adept (in the sense in which we now use the word) could repose long upon the nirvanic level; and He is far too highly evolved and far too unselfish to allow Himself to indulge in depression, however intensely He may feel the change when He returns to this grey, dull earth from worlds of unimagined splendour. Nevertheless the contrast is severe, and one who has found his true home in those higher worlds cannot but feel something of nostalgia while his duty compels him to dwell at the lower levels of ordinary life.

This has been spoken of as the great renunciation, and no doubt it is so; it would indeed be infinitely great if one who has reached that point did not retain the powers of the higher consciousness even while still functioning in the physical body. One who has reached the Asekha stage habitually carries His consciousness on the nirvanic level, even though He still possesses a physical body. I do not mean that He can be fully conscious on both the planes simultaneously. When He is actually writing a letter or conducting a conversation on the physical plane, His consciousness is centred there, just like that of the ordinary man, though the spiritual splendour is still present in the background; but the moment that His physical work is over, the consciousness naturally springs back again to its accustomed condition, and though He still sits in the same physical chair, though He is fully alive and alert to all that is going on around Him, He is in reality living on that higher level, and earthly objects, though still present to Him, are slightly out of focus. This being His condition, the retaining of the physical body is only a modified sacrifice, although it involves a good deal of annoyance in the way of waste of time in eating, dressing, and so on.

When a man definitely attains the astral consciousness he finds himself much less hampered along all the three lines which we have instanced. In the astral body he has no longer sense-organs, but he does not need them, for what in that world corresponds to our senses works without needing a specialised organ. Strictly speaking, the word sight is hardly applicable to the perception of things in the astral world; but that knowledge of surrounding objects which we gain by seeing them is as readily and much more perfectly acquired in that higher vehicle. Every particle of the astral body is responsive, though only to vibrations of its own sublevel; thus in that higher life we get the effect of seeing all round us simultaneously, instead of only in one direction.

Since, as has frequently been explained, all solid physical objects have counterparts of that lowest type of astral matter which corresponds on that plane to a solid, we see practically the same world around us when utilising the astral senses. But it is a far more populous world, for now we are able to see the millions of the sylphs or air-spirits, and also the hosts of the dead who have not yet risen above the astral level. Higher beings also are now within our purview, for we can see that lowest order of the Angel evolution which we have frequently called the desire-angels. All our friends who still have physical bodies remain just as visible to us as before, although we see only their astral vehicles; but now all their emotions and passions lie open before us, and it is no longer possible for the conventionalist to deceive us as to the real state of his feelings on any point. His thoughts, however, are still veiled, except in so far as they affect his feelings, and so show themselves through them.

The limitation of space has not yet disappeared, but its inconveniences are reduced to a minimum. We no longer need the clumsy methods of transportation with which we are familiar down here; the finer matter of this higher world responds so readily to the action of thought that merely to wish to be at any place is at once to begin to journey towards it. The journey still takes an appreciable time, even though the amount is small and we can reach the other side of the world in a few minutes. But the few minutes are necessary, and we still have the sensation of passing through space, and can check ourselves at any moment of our journey, so as to visit the intermediate countries.

The intellect is far freer here than in the lower world, as it has no longer to exhaust most of its strength in setting in motion the heavy and sluggish particles of the physical brain. We gain greatly also from the fact that fatigue has disappeared, so that we axe able to work steadily and continuously. Another advantage is that we are far less hampered at this level by pain and suffering. I do not mean that there is no suffering in the astral world; on the contrary, it may be in many ways more acute than it can be down here, but on the other hand it can much more readily be controlled. The astral world is the very home of passion and emotion, and therefore those who yield themselves to an emotion can experience it with a vigour and a keenness mercifully unknown on earth. Just as we have said that most of the strength of thought is spent in setting in motion the brain-particles, so most of the efficiency of any emotion is exhausted in transmission to the physical plane, so that all that we ever see down here is the remnant which is left of the real feeling, after all this work has been done by it. The whole of that force is available in its own world, and so it is possible there to feel a far more intense affection or devotion than we can ever gain amid the mists of earth. Naturally, the same thing is true with regard to the less pleasant emotions; accessions of hatred and envy, or waves of misery or fear, are a hundred times. more formidable on that plane than on this. So that the man who has no self-control is liable to experience an intensity of suffering which is unimaginable amidst the benignantly-imposed restrictions of common life.

The advantage is that, little as most people realise it, in the astral world all pain and suffering is in reality voluntary and absolutely under control, and that is why life at that level is so much easier for the man who understands. No doubt the power of mind over matter is wonderful in all the worlds, and even down here it frequently produces marvellous and unexpected results. But it is exceedingly difficult to control by the mind acute physical pain. I know that it can often be done from outside by mesmerism, or even by determined exertion along the lines of Christian Science, and that it is frequently done in India and elsewhere by yogis who have made a speciality of it; but the power so to control severe pain is not yet in the hands of most people, and even where it is possible, such an effort absorbs so much of the energy of the man as to leave him capable of little else for the time but holding the pain at bay.

The reason of this difficulty lies in the density of the matter; it is so far removed in level from the controlling forces that their hold on it is by no means secure, and great practice is required before definite results can be produced. The far finer astral matter responds immediately to an exertion of the will, so that while only the few can perfectly and instantly banish severe physical pain, everyone can in a moment drive away the suffering, caused by a strong emotion. The man has only to exert his will, and the passion straightway disappears. This assertion will sound startling to many; but a little thought will show that no man *need* be angry or jealous or envious; no man *need* allow himself to feel depression or fear; all these emotions are invariably the result of ignorance, and any man who chooses to make the effort can forth-with put them to flight.

In the physical world fear may sometimes have a certain amount of excuse, for it is undoubtedly possible for one who is more powerful than we to injure our physical bodies. But on the astral plane no one can do hurt to another, except indeed by employing methods congruous to the plane, which are always gradual in their operation and easy to be avoided. In this world a sudden blow may actually injure the texture of the physical body; but in the astral world all vehicles are fluidic, and a blow, a cut, or a perforation can produce no effect whatever, since the vehicle would close up again immediately, precisely as does water when a sword has passed through it.

It is the world of passions and emotions, and only through his passions and emotions can man be injured. A man may be corrupted, and persuaded to harbour evil passions, unworthy emotions; but these after all can be induced only slowly, and any man who wishes to resist them can do so with perfect ease. Therefore there is no reason whatever for fear upon the astral plane, and where it exists it is only through ignorance - ignorance which can be dispelled by a few moments' instruction and a little practice. Also, most of the reasons which cause suffering amid terrestrial surroundings are quite unrepresented. When we lay aside this body, there is no longer hunger or thirst, cold or heat, fatigue or sickness, poverty or riches; what room is there then for pain and suffering? One sees at a glance that that less material world cannot but be a happier one, for in that, far more than even in this, a man makes his own surroundings and can vary them at his will.

One of the greatest causes of suffering in our present life is what we are in the habit of calling our separation from those whom we love, when they leave their physical bodies behind them. Having only his physical consciousness, the uninstructed man supposes himself to have "lost" his departed friend; but this is really an illusion, for the departed friend stands beside him all the time, and watches the variations of feeling expressed in his astral body. It will at once be seen that it is impossible for the departed friend to be under any delusion that he has "lost" the loved ones who still retain physical vehicles, for since they must also possess astral bodies (or those physical vehicles could not live) the "dead" man has the living fully in sight all the time, though the consciousness of his living friend is available for the interchange of thought and sentiment only during the sleep of that friend's physical body. But at least the "dead" man has no sense of loneliness or separation, but has simply exchanged the day for the night as his time of companionship with those whom he loves who still belong to the lower world.

This most fertile source of sorrow is therefore entirely removed from one who possesses the astral consciousness. The man who has evolved to the point at which he is able to use fully both the astral and physical consciousness while still awake, can naturally never be separated from his departed friend, but has him present and fully available until the end of the latter's astral life, when that body in turn is dropped, and he enters upon his sojourn in the heaven-world. Then indeed an apparent separation does take place, though even then it can never be at all the same thing as what we call loss down here; for a man who has already fully realised the existence of two of the planes has thoroughly convinced himself of the plan of Nature's arrangements, and has a certainty with regard to them and a confidence in them which puts him in an altogether different position from the ignorance of the man who knows only one plane and cannot imagine anything beyond it.

In addition to this, a man who possesses astral consciousness has broken through the first and densest of the veils, and will find it no great effort to penetrate that which divides him from the mental world, so that it frequently happens that before the so-called "dead" person is ready to leave the astral plane, his friend has already opened the door of a yet higher consciousness, and is therefore able to accompany his "dead" associate in the next stage of his progress. Under any and all circumstances, and whether the man who is still in physical life is or is not conscious of what takes place, the apparent separation is never more than an illusion, for in the heaven-world the "dead" man makes for himself a thought-image of his friend, which is instantly observed and utilised by the ego of that friend; and in that way they are closer together than ever before.

Let us see what further advantages are gained by the man who has opened for himself the mental consciousness. Once again he passes through the experience already described, for he finds that this higher plane is thrilling with a glory and a bliss beside which even the wonderful vigour of the astral life pales its ineffectual fires. Once more he feels that now at last he has reached the true life, of which before he had only an inefficient and inaccurate reflection. Again his horizon is widened, for now the vast world of the Form-Angels opens before his astonished eyes. He sees now the whole of humanity - the enormous hosts who are out of incarnation as well as the comparatively few who possess vehicles upon the lower planes. Every man who is in physical or astral life must necessarily possess a mental body, and it is that which now represents him to the sight of the student who has come thus far on his way; but, in addition to this, the great army of those who are resting in the heaven-world is now within his view - though, as each is confined entirely within his own shell of thought, these men can hardly be regarded as in any sense of the word companions.

The visitor to their world can act upon them to the extent of flooding them with thoughts, say of affection. Sometimes these thoughts cannot so far penetrate the shell of the men who are enjoying their heaven-life as to carry with them any feeling of definite affection from the sender which could make them conscious of him, or evoke in them a reply directed personally towards him; but even then, the stream of affection can act upon the inhabitant of the heaven-world in precisely the same way as the warmth of the sun can operate upon the germ within the egg and hasten its fructification, or intensify whatever pleasurable sensations it may be supposed to have. Again, though these men in the heaven-world are not readily accessible to any influence from without, they are themselves pouring forth vibrations expressing the qualities most prominent in them; so the visitor to that world may bathe himself in such emanations as he chooses, and may go round selecting his type of emanation just as a visitor to Harrogate selects the variety of mineral water which he will drink, testing first one spring and then another.

Between those who are fully conscious on the mental plane there is a far closer union than has been possible at any lower level. A man can no longer deceive another with regard to what he thinks, for all mental operations lie open for every one to see. Opinions or impressions can now be exchanged not only with the quickness of thought but with perfect accuracy, for each now receives the exact idea of the other - clean, clear-cut, instantaneous - instead of having to try to puzzle his way to it through a jungle of inexpressive words. At this level a man may circle the world actually with the speed of thought; he is at the other side of it even as he formulates the wish to be there, for in this case the response of matter to thought is immediate, and the will can control it far more readily than on any lower level.

It has often been said in connection with meditation that there is much greater difficulty in governing thoughts than emotions, and that the mental elemental is less susceptible to control than the astral. For us down here this is usually so, but if we wish to understand the matter aright we must try to see why it is so. The physical body is along certain lines obedient to the action of the will, because we have carefully trained it to be so.

If we desire to lift an arm, we can lift it; if we desire to walk to a certain place, if the physical body is in health, we can get up and walk to it with no more resistance on the part of the body than the expression of its ordinary indolence or love of ease. When, however, the physical body has set up bad habits of any kind, it often proves exceedingly refractory and difficult to restrain. It is in such cases that the distance and difference in density between the controlling ego and its lowest vehicle becomes painfully evident. The management of the astral vehicle is in reality much easier, though many people find it difficult because they have never previously attempted it. The moment that one really thinks clearly of the matter this is obvious. It is not easy to banish by thought-power a raging toothache, though even that can be done under certain conditions; it is comparatively easy by thought-power to banish depression or anger or jealousy. The desire-elemental may be persistent in obtruding these feelings upon the man's notice; but at any rate they clearly are under his control; and by repeatedly throwing them off immunity from them can unquestionably be obtained.

Still more definitely is this true, and easier still ought to be our task, when we pass to the mental world. It seems to us more difficult to bridle thought than emotion because most of us have made at least some experiments in the direction of repressing emotion, and we have been taught from childhood that it is unseemly to allow it to display itself unchecked. On the other hand, we have been in the habit of allowing our thoughts to roam fancy-free, and it is probably only in connection with school lessons that we have reluctantly torn them back from their wanderings and tried to concentrate them on some definite task. To induce us to do even this much, exterior compulsion is usually required in the shape of constant exhortation from the teacher or the stimulus of emulation among our fellows in the class. It is because so little effort has been made by the average man in the direction of the regulation of thought that he finds it so difficult, and indeed almost impossible, when he begins the practice of meditation. He finds himself in conflict with the habits of the mental elemental, who has been used to have things all his own way, and to drift from subject to subject at his own sweet will.

Our struggle with him is in some ways different from that which we have already waged against the desire-elemental; and the reason for this will be obvious if we remember his constitution. He represents the downward-pouring life of the Solar Deity at the earliest stage of its immeshing in matte r- that which we usually call the First Elemental Kingdom. Consequently, he is less used to material confinement than is the desire-elemental, who belongs to a later kingdom, and is one whole stage lower down in the scale of matter. He is consequently more active than the desire-elemental - more restless, but less powerful and determined; he is in the nature of things easier to manage, but much less used to management; so that it takes far less actual exertion of strength to control a thought than a desire, but it needs a more persistent application of that strength. Remember that we are now at the level of thought, where literally thoughts are things; and this restive mental matter which we find so difficult to govern is the veryhome and definite vehicle of the mind with which we are to control it. That mind is here on its own ground and is dealing with its own matter, so that it is only a question of practice for it to learn to manage it perfectly; whereas, when we endeavour to rule the desire-elemental, we are bringing down the mind into a world which is foreign to it, and imposing an alien ascendency from without, so that we are badly equipped for the struggle.

To sum up then: control of mind is in itself far easier than control of the emotions, but we have had a certain amount of practice in the-latter, and as a rule almost no practice at all in the former; and it is for that reason only that the mental exercise seems so difficult to us. Both of them together constitute a far easier task than the perfect mastery of the physical body; but this latter we have been to some extent practising during a number of previous lives, though our achievements along that line are even yet notably imperfect. A thorough comprehension of this matter should be distinctly encouraging to the student; and the result of such comprehension is vividly to impress upon him the truth of the remark made in *The Voice of the Silence* that this earth is the only true hell which is known to the Occultist.

Let us now take one step farther, and turn our attention to the upper part of the mental plane, which is inhabited by the ego in his causal body. Now at last the veils have fallen away, and for the first time we meet man to man without possibility of misunderstanding. Even in the astral world the consciousness is already so different from that which we know down here, that it is practically impossible to give any coherent idea of it, and this difficulty increases as we attempt to deal with higher planes. Here thoughts no longer take form and float about as they do at lower levels, but pass like lightning-flashes from one soul to another. Here we have no newly-acquired vehicles, gradually coming under control and learning by degrees more or less feebly to express the soul within; but we are face to face with one body older than the hills, an actual expression of the Divine Glory which ever rests behind it, and shines through it more and more in the gradual unfolding of its powers. Here we deal no longer with outer forms, but we see the things in themselves - the reality which lies behind the imperfect expression. Here cause and effect are one, clearly visible in their unity, like two sides of the same coin. Here we have left the concrete for the abstract; we have no longer the multiplicity of forms, but the idea which lies behind all those forms.

Here the *essence* of everything is available; we no longer study details; we no longer talk round a subject or endeavour to explain it; we take up the essence or the idea of the subject and move it as a whole, as one moves a piece when playing chess. This is a world of realities, where not only is deception impossible but also unthinkable; we deal no longer with any emotions, ideas or conceptions, but with the thing in itself. It is impossible to express in words the ordinary traffic of ideas between men in fully-developed causal bodies. What down here would be a system of philosophy, needing many volumes to explain it, is there a single definite object - a thought which can be thrown down as one throws a card upon a table. An opera or an oratorio, which here would occupy a full orchestra for many hours in the rendering, is there a single mighty chord; the methods of a whole school of painting are condensed into one magnificent idea; and ideas such as these are the intellectual counters which are used by egos in their converse one with another.

There also we meet a higher order of Angels, more splendid but less comprehensible to our dull faculties. There for the first time we have fully unrolled before us all the stories of all the lives which have been lived upon our globe, the actual living records of the past; for this is the lowest plane on which the Divine Memory reflects itself. Here for the first time we see our lives as one vast whole, of which our descents into incarnation have been but the passing days. Here the great scheme of evolution is unfolded before us, so that we can see what is the Divine will for us.

The ordinary man is as yet but little developed as an ego; he needs the grosser matter of far lower planes in order to be able to sense vibrations and respond to them. But an ego who is awakened and is truly alive upon his own plane is indeed a glorious object, and gives us for the first time some idea of what God means man to be. The egos are still separate, yet intellectually they fully realise their inner unity, for they see one another as they are and can no longer blunder or fail to comprehend.

Strange as even that must seem when looked at from below, and far removed as it is from our ordinary conceptions of life, our next step brings us into a region even less possible to be grasped by the lower mind; for when we follow the man into the intuitional world, developing the buddhic consciousness, we are in the presence not only of an indefinite extension of various capacities, but also of an entire change of method. From the causal body we looked out upon everything, understanding, seeing everything exactly as it is and appraising it at its true value, yet still maintaining a distinction between subject and object, still conscious that we *looked upon* that which we so thoroughly comprehended. But now a change has come; the comprehension is more perfect and not less, but it is from within instead of from without. We no longer *look upon* a person or upon an object, no matter with what degree of kindliness or of sympathy; we simply *are* that person or that object, and we know him or it as we know the thought of our own brain or the movement of our own hand.

It is not easy even to suggest the subtle change which this casts over everything - the curiously different value which it gives to all the actions and relations of life. It is not only that we understand another man still more intimately; it is that we feel ourselves to be acting through him, and we appreciate his motives as our own motives, even though we may perfectly understand that another part of ourselves, possessing more knowledge or a different view-point, might act quite differently. All through our previous evolution we have had our own private view-point and our own qualities, which were cherished because they were our own - which seemed to us in some subtle way different from the same qualities when manifested in others; but now we lose entirely that sense of personal property in qualities and in ideas, because we see that these things are truly common to all, because they are part of the great reality which lies equally behind all. So personal pride in individual development becomes an utter impossibility, for we see now that personal development is but as the growth of one leaf among the thousands of leaves upon a tree, and that the important fact is not the size or shape of that particular leaf, but its relation to the tree as a whole; for it is only of the tree as a whole that we can really predicate permanent growth.

Down here we meet people of different dispositions; we study them, and we say to ourselves that under no conceivable circumstances could we ever act or think as they do, and though we sometimes talk of "putting ourselves in the other man's place", it is generally a feeble, half-hearted, insufficient substitution; but in the intuitional world we see clearly and instantly the reason for those actions which here seem so incomprehensible and repugnant, and we readily understand that it is we ourselves in another form who are doing those very things which seem to us so reprehensible, and we recognise that to that facet of ourselves such action is quite right and natural. We find that we have ceased altogether to blame others for their differences from ourselves; we simply note them as other manifestations of our own activity, for now we see reasons which before were hidden from us. Even the evil man is clearly seen to be part of ourselves - a weak part; so our desire is not to blame him, but to help him by pouring strength into that weak part of ourselves, so that the whole body of humanity may be vigorous and healthy.

When in the causal body, we already recognised the Divine Consciousness in all; when we looked upon another ego, that consciousness leaped up in him to recognise the Divine within us. Now it no longer leaps to greet us from without, for it is already enshrined within our hearts. We *are* that consciousness and it is *our* consciousness. There is no longer the "you" and the "I", for we both are one - both facets of something that transcends and yet includes us both.

Yet in all this strange advance there is no loss of the sense of individuality, even though there is an utter loss of the sense of separateness. That seems a paradox, yet it is obviously true. The man remembers all that lies behind him. He is himself, the same man who did this action or that in the far-off past. He is in no way changed, except that now he is much more than he was then, and feels that he includes within himself many other manifestations as well. If here and now a hundred of us could simultaneously raise our consciousness into the intuitional world, we should all be one consciousness, but to each man that would seem to be his own, absolutely unchanged except that now it included all the others as well.

To each it would seem that it was *he* who had absorbed or included all those others; so we are here manifestly in the presence of a kind of illusion, and a little further realisation makes it clear to us that we are all facets of a greater consciousness, and that what we have hitherto thought to be our qualities, our intellect, our energy, have all the time been His qualities, His intellect, His energy. We have arrived at the realisation in actual fact of the time-honoured formula: "Thou art that". It is one thing to talk about this down here and to grasp it, or think that we grasp it, intellectually; but it is quite another to enter into that marvellous world and *know* it with a certainty that can never again be shaken.

Yet it must not be supposed that when a man enters upon the lowest subdivision of that world, he at once becomes fully conscious of his unity with all that lives. That perfection of sense comes only as the result of much toil and trouble, when he has reached the highest subdivision of this realm of unity. To enter that plane at all is to experience an enormous extension of consciousness, to realise himself as one with many others; but before him then there opens a time of effort, a time of self-development, analogous at that level to what we do down here when by meditation we try to open our consciousness to the plane next above us. Step by step, sub-plane by sub-plane, the aspirant wins his way; for even at that level exertion is still necessary if progress is to be made.

A stage below this, while we were still in the higher mental plane, we learned to see things as they are, to get behind our preconceptions of them, and to reach the reality which lay behind what we had been able to see of them. Now we are able to see the reality which lay behind other people's divergent views of that same object; coming simultaneously up their lines as well as our own, we enter into that thing and we realise all its possibilities, because now it is ourselves, and its possibilities are possible also for us. Difficult to put into words; impossible fully to comprehend down here; and yet approaching and hinting at a truth which is more real than what we call reality in this world.

If we could instantly be transported to that level without passing slowly through the intermediate stages, most of what we found ourselves able to see would mean but little to us. To change abruptly even into the astral consciousness gives one so different an outlook that many familiar objects are entirely unrecognisable. Such a thing, for example, as a book or a water-bottle presents to us a certain appearance with which we are familiar; but if we suddenly find ourselves able to see that object from all sides at once, as well as from above and below, we shall perhaps realise that it presents an appearance so different that we should require a considerable amount of mental adjustment before we could name it with certainty. Add to that the further complication that the whole inside of the body is laid out before us as though every particle were separately placed upon a table, and we shall again see that additional difficulties are introduced. Add to them again yet another fact - that while we look upon all these particles as described, we are yet at the same time within each of those particles and are looking out through it, and we shall see that it becomes an absolute impossibility to trace any resemblance to the object which we knew in the physical world.

That is, of course, nothing but an illustration - a coarse and concrete example of what takes place; and in order really to understand, one must spiritualise it and add to it many other considerations - all of which, however, tend to make the recognition more difficult rather than less. Fortunately in nature no sudden leap of this kind is possible. The method of evolution is gradual unfoldment, so that we are led on little by little until we are able to face without flinching glories which would dazzle us if they burst unexpectedly upon our view.

At this level man still has a definite body, and yet his consciousness seems equally present in vast numbers of other bodies. The web of life (which, you know, is constructed of buddhic matter - matter of the intuitional world) is extended so that it includes these other people, so that instead of many small separate webs we get one vast web which enfolds them all in one common life. But remember that many of these others may be entirely unconscious of this change, and to them their own private little part of the web will still seem as much separated as ever - or *would* do so if they knew anything at all about the web of life. So from this standpoint and at this level it seems that all mankind are bound together thus by golden threads, and make one complex unit, no longer a man, but man in the abstract.

What can we say of the next stage of consciousness, that which has often been called nirvana? This noble word has been translated to mean annihilation, but nothing could be further from the truth than this, for it represents the most intense and vivid life of which we know anything. Perhaps it may not unfairly be described as annihilation of all that we on the physical plane know and think of as the man; for all his personality, all his lower qualities, have long ago utterly disappeared. Yet the essence is there; the true man is there; the Divine Spark, descended from the Deity Himself, is still there, though now it has grown into a Flame - a Flame that is becoming consciously part of That from which it came; for here all consciousness merges into Him, even though it still retains all that was best in the feeling of individuality. The man still feels himself, just as he does now, but full of a delight, a vigour, a capacity, for which we have simply no words down here. He has in no way lost his personal memories. He is just as much himself as ever, only it is a wider self. He still knows that "I am I"; but he also realises, and far more prominently, that "I am He".

In the intuitional world his consciousness had widened so as to take in that of many other people. Now it seems to include the entire spiritual world, and the man feels that he is on the way to realising the divine attribute of omnipresence; for he exists not only in all those others, but also at every point of the intervening space, so that he can focus himself wherever he will, thus realising exactly the well-known phrase that he is a circle whose centre is everywhere and its circumference nowhere. He has transcended intellect as we know it, yet he knows and understands far more fully than ever before. On lower planes (lower than this, yet to us high beyond all reaching) he has seen the great Angels and Archangels in all their glorious order. In this spiritual world he comes face to face with the powers that rule, with the great Administrators of Karma, with the great Leaders of the Occult Hierarchy; with Planetary Spirits of stupendous power and wondrous beauty.

It is hopeless to attempt to describe this life which transcends all life that we know, and yet is so utterly different from it as to seem almost a negation of it - a splendour of purposeful life as compared with a mere blind crawling along darkened ways. For this indeed is life and this is reality, as far as we can reach it at present; although we doubt not for a moment that beyond even this indescribable glory there extend yet greater glories which surpass it even as it surpasses this catacomb life of earth. There, all is God, and all these august Beings are obviously great manifestations of Him; and so thoroughly is this conviction borne in upon a man's consciousness, so entirely does it become part of him, that when he descends once more to the physical globe of this sorrowful star he cannot forget it, but ever thereafter he sees the Divine Spark, even in the most unlikely surroundings. Down here it is often hard to recognise; we need to dig so deeply in order to find it. In that spiritual world it is self-evident, and we know, because we see it, that there is nothing but God - no life anywhere in all the worlds but the Divine Life.

For at that level the man himself has become as a god among gods, a lesser light among the greater lights, yet truly an orb of splendour, even though so much less than the Masters, than the Great Devas, than the Mighty Spirits who rule the destinies of men and worlds. There we see face to face all these great Beings of whom down here we hear and read, of whom sometimes we make faint images. There we see with open face the beauty of which down here we can but catch the faintest reflections. There we hear the glorious music of the spheres, of which only occasional echoes can reach us in this lower world.

Truly terrible as is the descent from that great world to this, yet one who has once touched that consciousness can never again be the same as he was before. He cannot wholly forget, even amidst the darkness and the storm, that his eyes have seen the King in His beauty, that he has beheld the land which is very far off, and yet at the same time is near, even at our doors, close about us all the while, if we will but lift up our eyes to see it, if we will but develop the God within us till He can respond to the God without.

"The land which is very far off"; from the days of our childhood the phrase has been familiar to us, and it falls upon our ears with all the magic of holy associations; yet it is a mistranslation of the original Hebrew, and perhaps the real meaning of the text is even more beautiful and more appropriate, for the expression which Isaiah used is "the land of far distances", as though he were contrasting in his mind the splendid spaciousness of the star-strewn fields of heaven with the noisome narrowness of the cramped catacombs of earth. Yet even here and now, imprisoned in densest matter, we may lift our thoughts to the sun, for when once we know the truth, the truth has made us free. When once we have realised our unity with God, no darkness can ever shade us again, for we know that He is Light of Light, and the Father of Lights, with whom is no variableness, neither shadow of turning; and in Him is no darkness at all.

All this knowledge, all this glory, is within our reach, and must inevitably come to every one of us in the course of our evolution, as surely as day follows night. It is beyond all words now, beyond all feelings - beyond our intuition even. But there will come a time when we shall know even as now also we are known. All that will come to us in the course of nature (in the seventh round, as we have said), even though we drift along and make no exertion; but far earlier if we are willing to undertake the labour which earns it - hard work indeed, yet noble work and pleasant in the doing, even though at times it may bring with it much of suffering. Yet the way is the Way of Service, and each step that we take is taken not for ourselves but for others, that through our realisation others may realise, that through our exertion others may find the Path, that through the blessing which comes to us the whole world may also be blessed.

THE BUDDHIC CONSCIOUSNESS

Much has been written about the buddhic or intuitional world, and all students are theoretically acquainted with its wonderful characteristic of unity of consciousness; but most of them probably regard the possibility of obtaining any personal experience of that consciousness as belonging to the far-distant future. The full development of the buddhic vehicle is for most of us still remote, for it belongs to the stage of the Fourth or Arhat Initiation; but it is perhaps not entirely impossible for those who are as yet far from that level to gain some touch of that higher type of consciousness in quite another way.

I was myself brought along what I should describe as the ordinary and commonplace line of occult development, and I had to fight my way laboriously upward, conquering one sub-plane after another, first in the astral world, then in the mental, and then in the buddhic; which means that I had the full use of my astral, mental and causal vehicles before anything came to me that I could define certainly as a real buddhic experience. This method is slow and toilsome, though I think it has its advantages in developing accuracy in observation, in making sure of each step before the next is taken. I have no doubt whatever that it was the best for a person of my temperament; indeed, it was probably the only way possible for me; but it does rot follow that other people may not have quite other opportunities.

It has happened to me in the course of my work to come into contact with a number of those who are undergoing occult training; and perhaps the fact which emerges most prominently from my experience in that direction is the marvellous variety of method employed by our Masters. So closely adapted is the training to the individual, that in no two cases is it the same; not only has every Master His own plan, but the same Master adopts a different scheme for each pupil, and so each person is brought along exactly that line which is most suitable for him.

A remarkable instance of this variability of method came under my notice not long ago, and I think that an explanation of it may perhaps be useful to some of our students. Let me first remind them of the curious inverted way in which the ego is reflected in the personality; the higher *manas* or intellect images itself in the mental body, the intuition or *buddhi* reflects itself in the astral body, and the spirit or *atma* itself somehow corresponds to the physical. These correspondences show themselves in the three methods of individualisation, and they play their part in certain inner developments; but until lately it had not occurred to me that they could be turned to practical account at a much earlier stage by the aspirant for occult progress.

A certain student of deeply affectionate nature developed an intense love for the teacher who had been appointed by his Master to assist him in the preliminary training. He made it a daily practice to form a strong mental image of that teacher, and then pour out his love upon him with all his force, thereby flooding his own astral body with crimson, and temporarily increasing its size enormously. He used to call the process "enlarging his aura". He showed such remarkable aptitude in this exercise, and it was so obviously beneficial to him, that an additional effort along the same line was suggested to him. He was recommended, while holding the image clearly before him, and sending out the love-force as strongly as ever, to try to raise his consciousness to a higher level and unify it with that of his teacher.

His first attempt to do this was amazingly successful. He described a sensation as of actually rising through space; he found what he supposed to be the sky like a roof barring his way, but the force of his will seemed to form a sort of cone in it, which presently became a tube through which he found himself rushing. He emerged into a region of blinding light which was at the same time a sea of bliss so overwhelming that he could find no words to describe it. It was not in the least like anything that he had ever felt before; it grasped him as definitely and instantaneously as a giant hand might have done, and permeated his whole nature in a moment like a flood of electricity. It was more real than any physical object that he had ever seen, and yet at the same time so utterly spiritual. "It was as though GOD had taken me into Himself, and I felt His Life running through me", he said.

He gradually recovered himself and was able to examine his condition; and as he did so he began to realise that his consciousness was no longer limited as it had hitherto been - that he was somehow simultaneously present at every point of that marvellous sea of light; indeed, that in some inexplicable way he was himself that sea, even though apparently at the same time he was a point floating in it. It seemed to us who heard, that he was groping after words to express the consciousness which, as Madame Blavatsky so well puts it, has "its centre everywhere and its circumference nowhere".

Further realisation revealed to him that he had succeeded in his effort to become one with the consciousness of his teacher. He found himself thoroughly comprehending and sharing that teacher's feelings, and possessing a far wider and higher outlook on life than he had ever had before. One thing that impressed him immensely was the image of himself as seen through the teacher's eyes; it filled him with a sense of unworthiness, and yet of high resolve; as he whimsically put it:

"I found myself loving myself through my teacher's intense love for me, and I knew that I could and would make myself worthy of it."

He sensed also a depth of devotion and reverence which he had never before reached; he knew that in becoming one with his earthly teacher he had also entered the shrine of his true Master, with whom that teacher in turn was one, and he dimly felt himself in touch with a Consciousness of unrealisable splendour. But here his strength failed him; he seemed to slide down his tube again, and opened his eyes upon the physical plane.

Consulted as to this transcendent experience, I enquired minutely into it, and easily satisfied myself that it was unquestionably an entry into the buddhic world, not by toilsome progress through the various stages of the mental, but by a direct course along the ray of reflection from the highest astral sub-plane to the lowest of that intuitional world. I asked as to the physical effects, and found that there were absolutely none; the student was in radiant health. So I recommended that he should repeat the effort, and that he should with utmost reverence try to press higher still, and to raise himself, if it might be, into that other August Consciousness. For I saw that here was a case of that combination of golden love and iron will that is so rare on this our Sorrowful Star; and I knew that a love which is utterly unselfish and a will which recognises no obstacles may carry their possessor to the very Feet of GOD Himself.

The student repeated his experiment, and again he succeeded beyond all hope or expectation. He was able to enter that wider Consciousness, and he pressed onward and upward into it as though he were swimming out into some vast lake. Much of what he brought back with him he could not comprehend; shreds of ineffable glories, fragments of conceptions so vast and so gorgeous that no merely human mind can grasp them in their totality. But he gained a new idea of what love and devotion could be - an ideal after which to strive for the rest of his life.

Day after day he continued his efforts (we found that once a day was as often as it could be wisely attempted); further and further he penetrated into that great lake of love, and yet found no end to it. But gradually he became aware of something far greater still; he somehow knew that this indescribable splendour was permeated by a subtler glory yet more inconceivably splendid, and he tried to raise himself into that. And when he succeeded he knew by its characteristics that this was the Consciousness of the great World-Teacher Himself. In becoming one with his own earthly teacher he had inevitably joined himself to the consciousness of his Master, with whom that teacher was already united; and in this further marvellous experience he was but proving the close union which exists between that Master and the Bodhisattva, Who in turn had taught Him. Into that shoreless sea of Love and Compassion he plunges daily in his meditation, with such upliftment and strengthening for himself as may readily be imagined; but he can never reach its limits, for no mortal man can fathom such an ocean as that.

Striving ever to penetrate more and more deeply into this wondrous new realm which had so suddenly opened before him, he succeeded one day in reaching a yet further development - a bliss so much more intense, a feeling so much more profound, that it seemed to him at first as much higher than his first buddhic touch as that had been above his earlier astral experiences. He remarked:

"If I did not know that it is impossible for me to attain it yet, I should say that this must be Nirvana."

In reality it was only the next sub-plane of the buddhic - the second from the bottom, and the sixth from the top; but his impression is significant as showing that not only does consciousness widen as we rise, but the rate at which it widens increases rapidly. Not only is progress accelerated, but the rate of such acceleration grows by geometrical progression. Now this student reaches that higher sub-plane daily and as a matter of course, and is working vigorously and perseveringly in the hope of advancing still farther. And the power, the balance and the certainty which this introduces into his daily physical life is amazing and beautiful to see.

Another phenomenon which he observes, as accompanying this, is that the intense bliss of that higher plane now persists beyond the time of meditation and is becoming more and more a part of his whole life. At first this persistence was for some twenty minutes after each meditation; then it reached an hour; then two hours; and he is confidently looking forward to a time when it will be his as a permanent possession - a part of himself. A remarkable feature of the case is that this prodigious daily exaltation is not followed by any sign of the slightest reaction or depression, but instead produces an ever-augmenting radiance and sunniness.

Becoming gradually more accustomed to functioning in this higher and more glorious world, he began to look about him to some extent, and was presently able to identify himself with many other less exalted consciousnesses. He found these existing as points within his extended self, and he discovered that by focusing himself at any one of these points he could at once realise the highest qualities and spiritual aspirations of the person whom it represented. Seeking for a more detailed sympathy with some whom he knew and loved, he discerned that these points of consciousness were also, as he put it, holes through which he could pour himself down into their lower vehicles; and thus he came into touch with those parts of their lives and dispositions which could find no expression on the buddhic plane. This gave him a sympathy with the characters, a comprehension of their weaknesses, which was truly remarkable, and could probably have been attained in no other way - a most valuable quality for the work of a disciple in the future.

The wondrous unity of that intuitional world manifested itself to him in unsuspected examples. Holding in his hand one day what he regarded as a specially beautiful little object, part of which was white, he fell into a sort of ecstasy of admiration of its graceful form and harmonious colouring. Suddenly, through the object, as he gazed at it, he saw unfolded before him a landscape, just as though the object had become a tiny window, or perhaps a crystal. The landscape is one that he knows and loves well, but there was no obvious reason why the little object should bring it thus before him. A curious feature was that the white part of that object was represented in the landscape by huge piles of cumulus clouds, which he saw as floating in the sky of his picture.

Impressed by this wholly unexpected phenomenon, he tried the experiment of raising his consciousness while he revelled in the beauty of the prospect. He had the sensation of passing through some resisting medium into a higher plane, and found that the view before him had changed to one which was strange to him, but even more beautiful than that which he knew so well. The piles of white cloud had become a towering snow-covered mountain, with its long line sweeping down to a sea of colour richer than any that in this incarnation he had seen. The rocky bays, the buildings, the vegetation, were all foreign to him, though well-known to me; and by a little careful questioning I soon ascertained without room for doubt that the scene upon which he was looking was that which I suspected - a real physical view, but one many thousands of miles from the spot where he sat gazing at it. Since that hallowed spot is often in my mind, though I was not thinking of it at that moment, what the student saw may have been a thought-form of mine.

I imagine that up to this point what had happened may be quite simply described. I presume that the student's emotion was excited by his admiration, and that the heightened vibrations which were caused in this way brought into operation his astral senses, and this enabled him to see a view which was not physically visible, but well within astral reach. The endeavour to press on further temporarily opened the mental sense, and by it he was able to see my thought-form-if that second view was a thought-form of mine.

But the student did not rest satisfied with that; he repeated his attempt to push on still higher, or as he put it, still deeper into the real meaning of it all. Once more he had the experience of breaking through into some more exalted and more refined state of matter; and this time it was no earthly scene that rewarded his effort, for the foreground burgeoned forth into an illimitable universe filled with masses of splendid colour, pulsating with glorious life, and the snow-covered mountain became a great White Throne vaster than any mountain, veiled in dazzling golden light.

A strange fact connected with this vision is that the student to whom the experience came is entirely unacquainted with the Christian scripture, and was unaware that any text existing therein had any bearing upon what he saw. I asked him whether he could repeat this experience at will; he did not know, but later on he tried the experiment, and succeeded in passing again through those stages in the same order, giving some additional details of the foreign landscape which proved to me that this was not merely a feat of memory; and this time the awestricken seer whispered that amidst the coruscations of that light he once had a passing glimpse of the outline of a Mighty Figure Who sat upon the Throne. This also, you may say, might be a thought-form, built by some Christian of vivid imagination. Perhaps; but when a few days later an opportunity occurred, and I asked a Wise One what signification we might attach to such a vision, He replied:

"Do you not see that, as there is but One Love, so there is but One Beauty? Whatever is beautiful, on any plane, is so because it is part of that Beauty, and if it is pushed back far enough, its connection will become manifest. All Beauty is of GOD, as all Love is of GOD; and through these His Qualities the pure in heart may always reach Him."

Our students would do well to weigh these words, and follow out the idea contained in them. All beauty, whether it be of form or of colour, whether it be in nature or in the human frame, in high achievements of art or in the humblest household utensil, is but an expression of the One Beauty; and therefore in even the lowliest thing that is beautiful all beauty is implicitly contained, and so through it all beauty may be realised, and He Who Himself is Beauty may be reached. To understand this fully needs the buddhic consciousness by which our student arrived at its realisation; but even at much lower levels the idea may be useful and fruitful.

I fully admit that the student whose experiences I have been relating is exceptional - that he possesses a strength of will, a power of love, a purity of heart and an utter unselfishness which are, unfortunately, far from common. Nevertheless, what he has done with such marked success may surely be copied to some extent by others less gifted. He has unfolded his consciousness upon a plane which is not normally reached by aspirants; he is rapidly building for himself a capable and most valuable vehicle there - for that is the meaning of the ever-increasing persistence of the sense of bliss and power. That his is a definite line of progress, and not a mere isolated example, is shown by the fact that even already the abnormal buddhic development is producing its effect upon the apparently neglected causal and mental bodies, stimulating them into action from above instead of leaving them to be laboriously influenced from below as is usual. All this success is the result of steady effort along the line which I have described.

"Go thou and do likewise." No harm can come to any man from an earnest endeavour to increase his power of love, his power of devotion, and his power to appreciate beauty; and by such endeavour it is at least possible that he may attain a progress of which he has not dreamed. Only be it remembered that, in this path as in every other, growth is achieved only by him who desires it not for his own sake, but for the sake of service. Forgetfulness of self and an eager desire to help others are the most prominent characteristics of the student whose inner story I have here told; these characteristics *must* be equally prominent in any who aspire to follow his example; without them no such consummation is possible.

www.ingramcontent.com/pod-product-compliance
Lightning Source LLC
LaVergne TN
LVHW041501070426
835507LV00009B/734